I SAID THIS YOU HEARD THAT

HOW YOUR WIRING
COLORS YOUR COMMUNICATION

KATHLEEN EDELMAN
FOREWORD BY ANDY STANLEY

© 2018 by North Point Ministries, Inc.

Interior layout and design by Fleecher Designs, LLC (fleecherdesigns.com).

Italics in Scripture quotations are the author's emphasis. Scripture quotations are from: The Holy Bible, New International Version (NIV) © 1973, 1978, 1984, 2011 by Biblica, Inc.™ Used by permission. All rights reserved worldwide.

Printed in Canada

CONTENTS

DEDICATION

To My Children:

Avery (my sanguine): You remind me daily to stop, be present, and enjoy the wonder of life. I love that you look at the best in every person and the beauty of the world around you.

Brice (my melancholic): You remind me every day of the importance of balance and how the differences in the world can bring us together. I love that you can be quiet, funny, and deeply compassionate at the same time you are smart, strong, and influential.

Though words hold so much power, there will never be the correct ones to fully express the depth, intensity, and fierceness of my love for both of you.

Be true to yourself, consistent in character, and authentically who God designed you to be.

I love you,

Mom

AVERY AND BRICE, 2003

FOREWORD

When I empty the dishwasher, I make as much noise as possible.

Why?

I want to make sure my wife, Sandra, hears how "helpful" I'm being.

Why?

What is it that makes me crave credit? Kathleen Edelman would tell you it's my temperament.

I was introduced to Kathleen a few years ago when she taught a training session for foster parents. (Sandra and I are the proud foster parents of a now 18-year-old daughter.) In that session, Kathleen explained that we're each wired with a specific set of needs. Some of us need affection, some need harmony, and some need credit for their work.

And that got me thinking about Sandra and the dishwasher.

It's true that some words seem to scratch an itch. They're so satisfying that I'll go out of my way to hear them. Kathleen encouraged us to figure out what those words were for our foster kids and to be intentional about saying them. It was the same advice I'd heard from someone else—the apostle Paul. Two thousand years ago, he said:

Do not let any unwholesome talk come out of your mouths, but only what is helpful for building others up according to their needs, that it may benefit those who listen.

Ephesians 4:29

In this verse, Paul tells us that when we're speaking to others, we should prioritize *their* needs. Usually, we're trying to make our point, win an argument, get the last word in, or just sound smart. Paul flips the script and tells us that instead of using words to build ourselves up, we should build *others* up.

I've preached on this idea dozens of times over the years. But *knowing what to do* is one thing, and *doing it* is something else entirely. *I Said This, You Heard That* is the most practical tool I've seen for turning Ephesians 4:29 into something I can actually do.

Kathleen's step-by-step approach has been a game-changer for me as a father, a husband, and a boss.

By pairing one powerful sentence from the apostle Paul with a framework that can be applied to anyone, Kathleen will have you "building others up" with your words and maybe rethinking every conversation you've ever had.

Andy Stanley

FROM THE AUTHOR

Thirty years ago, an audiocassette tape changed my life.

My husband and I were newly married, moving from California to Maryland. To keep us entertained on the long cross-country drive, I brought a stash of tapes, including one from Florence Littauer, the author of a book called *Personality Plus*.

By the time we reached our destination, Florence had changed the entire course of my career. Her talk introduced me to the ideas you'll encounter in this study, and I simply couldn't get enough. I immediately went back to school. I've spent the decades since teaching individuals, couples, families, and teams about how their wiring affects their communication. In that time, I've witnessed thousands of *aha* moments—lightning bolts of understanding that have changed lives and relationships *forever*.

As you're about to see, this is a six-part study, but it's really just the beginning of a *lifelong* journey. Thanks for coming along.

Kathleen Edelman

FROM FLORENCE LITTAUER

Kathleen and I share a passion for teaching the temperaments because we both deeply believe that understanding your God-given wiring will help you amplify your strengths and overcome your weaknesses. But I think you'll find the even more powerful thing about this framework is how it improves your relationships. I've seen it in my life and in the lives of thousands I've encountered for decades while writing, counseling, and speaking about this topic. I'm so proud of Kathleen's commitment to this material and am thrilled she's now made it so accessible.

HOW TO USE THE WORKBOOK

ARE YOU THE LEADER OR FACILITATOR?

If you are leading a group of friends or your Bible study group through this study, check out

ISAIDYOUHEARD.STUDY/LEADER

for tips on how to lead the discussion for each session.

HOW TO USE THIS STUDY IN A GROUP

1 ▶ WATCH.

As a group, watch the session video, viewable from the *I Said This, You Heard That* app or DVD.

2 ▶ DISCUSS.

As a group, talk through the Discussion Questions found at the beginning of each chapter.

3 ▶ DIG IN.

On your own, review the weekly reading and complete the homework activities before your group meets again.

GET THE FREE APP

Watch the six videos on your phone, tablet, or TV.
Search for *I Said This, You Heard That.*

Also available on **ROKU**

AN INTRODUCTION TO THE TEMPERAMENTS

HOW TO USE TABS

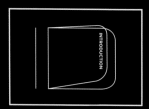

POP OUT TAB

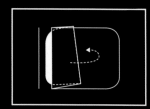

FOLD TAB BACK

This side of tab will show on reverse.

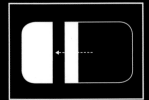

INSERT TAB THROUGH SLIT

Session One

AN INTRODUCTION TO THE TEMPERAMENTS

Session One at a Glance

During Session One...

1 Watch the Session One video (13 minutes).

2 Discuss the session questions.

3 Complete the Temperaments Assessment.
Or you can make this something you complete individually outside of group.

Homework...

4 Read pages 13–16.

VIDEO NOTES

DISCUSSION QUESTIONS

1 ▶ Have you ever made a resolution or tried to break a habit related to your words? Was it easy or hard?

2 ▶ What are some of the words—positive or negative—you remember being spoken to you as a child?

3 ▶ Talk about a time someone wrote or spoke words that built you up.

4 ▶ Has anything (e.g., a book, sermon, personality profile, or wise principle) helped improve your communication with others?

5 ▶ Why do you think God cares about our words? For example, here are just a few of the many warnings recorded in Proverbs, known as the book of wisdom.

   • *The tongue has the power of life and death.* (Proverbs 18:21)
   • *Those who guard their lips preserve their lives, but those who speak rashly will come to ruin.* (Proverbs 13:3)
   • *The one who has knowledge uses words with restraint.* (Proverbs 17:27)

6 ▶ Let's identify your temperament. The assessment will take around 20 minutes to complete. If time permits, go ahead and take the assessment individually right now—*during* your group gathering. (It begins on page 23.) If not, be sure to complete it on your own *before* your next gathering.

HOMEWORK

▶ Read pages 13–16.

▶ Take the assessment (if you didn't have the chance to complete it during your group session). It begins on page 23 and should take approximately 20 minutes to complete.

DO NOT LET ANY
UNWHOLESOME
TALK COME OUT
OF YOUR MOUTHS,
BUT ONLY WHAT
IS HELPFUL FOR
BUILDING OTHERS
UP ACCORDING TO
THEIR NEEDS, THAT
IT MAY BENEFIT
THOSE WHO LISTEN.

Ephesians 4:29

SESSION READING

Words are powerful.

They create (and destroy) confidence.
They start (and wreck) relationships.
They land (and lose) jobs.

You've probably felt the sting of a careless comment from your parent or experienced the hurtful teasing of a classmate on the playground. And you've likely whispered gossip you wish you could take back or said something in the heat of the moment you regretted when the argument had passed. On the brighter side, a charming remark may have led you to love, or praise from your boss may have been a turning point in your career.

For better and, unfortunately, for worse, the words you say and the words you hear have the power to shape your entire life.

And the more sobering thing—the reason for this study—is that your words have the power to shape other people's lives too. Every day, with every word, you can build up or tear down.

The apostle Paul knew this. (Maybe he'd learned it the hard way like so many of us.) So when he wrote a letter to a church he had founded years earlier in Ephesus, Paul reminded them to watch their words. His advice:

DO NOT LET ANY UNWHOLESOME TALK COME OUT OF YOUR MOUTHS, BUT ONLY WHAT IS HELPFUL FOR BUILDING OTHERS UP ACCORDING TO THEIR NEEDS, THAT IT MAY BENEFIT THOSE WHO LISTEN.

Ephesians 4:29

Paul was sharing the same truth we're looking at—that your words can help or hurt. His advice was to choose the helpful words. Of course, we'd all agree. The problem is we just keep messing it up! Wanting to help, not hurt, with our words doesn't seem to be enough. We need to get practical.

That's what we'll do over the next five sessions. You'll start by learning how you are uniquely wired to say and hear certain words. Then you'll figure out the words others are wired for and practice avoiding the hurtful ones and choosing the helpful ones. The framework we'll use is the four temperaments. Let's take a high-level look at it now.

THE FOUR TEMPERAMENTS FRAMEWORK

History

Hundreds of years before Jesus lived, the father of medicine, Hippocrates, described four categories of human traits and behavior that he believed were influenced by the "humors," or the four elemental fluids of the body. Later, Greek physician and philosopher Galen named these categories and applied them to his study of human temperament. The original Greek names were Sanguine (blood), Choleric (yellow bile), Melancholic (black bile), and Phlegmatic (phlegm).

More than two thousand years later, these classifications continue to be leveraged in modern psychology, influencing the work of Sigmund Freud and Carl Jung and forming the basis of personality profiles like Myers-Briggs™ and RightPath™.

Temperament vs. Personality

Over the next five sessions, we're going to look at temperament, not personality. So let's be clear on the difference between the two.

Temperament is your innate wiring from God—what you're naturally predisposed to. Like your eye color or fingerprint, it's unchangeable. It's why some people are drawn to the spotlight and stage and others are content with a cubicle in a quiet office. You don't choose who you are and you can't change how you're wired... though many of us try. (We'll get to that later.)

Personality is how you display your thoughts and feelings. It's influenced by things like birth order, education, and experiences. It can, and does, evolve over time. Just think about the high school version of you compared to the man or woman you are today. The years and experiences in-between have changed you.

> YOUR TEMPERAMENT IS THE `WHY` BEHIND YOUR PERSONALITY.

MEET THE FOUR TEMPERAMENTS

There are four temperaments, each predisposed to speak (and hear) certain words. It may be helpful to think of your temperament as your first (or native) language. It's what comes naturally to you. When someone engages you in conversation, responding in this language is automatic; you do not even have to think about it.

SANGUINES

SPEAK

The Language of
People & Fun

CHOLERICS

SPEAK

The Language of
Power & Control

PHLEGMATICS

SPEAK

The Language of
Calm & Harmony

MELANCHOLICS

SPEAK

The Language of
Perfection & Order

What Language Do You Speak?

You may already be guessing what your temperament is. The following pages have an assessment for you to take.

This is a big step toward a whole new way to use words.

YOU HAVE AN OPPORTUNITY EVERY DAY, WITH EVERY PERSON YOU ENCOUNTER, TO HURT OR TO HELP.

It's obvious which one you want to do. You just need the practical tools to do it. That's what you'll get in the temperaments framework.

By the end of this study, you'll know:

- The words you need to hear from others.
- The words your loved ones need from you.
- The words you're most likely to use as weapons.
- The words that will wound your loved ones.

You're on your way to knowing how your wiring colors your communcation. Let's keep going by figuring out your temperament.

WHAT'S MY TEMPERAMENT?

An Assessment to Determine Your Wiring

The following assessment contains 40 questions and takes approximately 20 minutes to complete. No temperament is better than any other, so **answer as honestly as you can based on how you typically think or behave**—not how you want others to see you. Just relax and follow your first instinct.

Watch a 1-minute video tutorial on how to complete this assessment. Look for it on the "Extras" tab of the *I Said This, You Heard That* mobile app.

DIRECTIONS

In order to easily calculate your results at the end, write your answers for all questions on the lines in the Scoring Column on the far right.

Example: 1. **A.** Ready to jump into new tasks, energized by challenges
B. Agreeable, easy to get along with
C. Sensitive to the emotions of others
D. Excitable, passionate, quick to say yes

1.	C
2.	
3.	

QUESTIONS

Choose the ONE description you most naturally identify with.
Ask yourself: *Am I someone who (is)...*

1. **A.** Ready to jump into new tasks, energized by challenges
   B. Agreeable, easy to get along with
   C. Sensitive to the emotions of others
   D. Excitable, passionate, quick to say yes

2. **A.** Motivated to achieve goals, eager to be the leader
   B. Energetic, lively, exhibits love and affection openly
   C. Logical, gathers facts and data, likes lists
   D. Flexible, able to adjust to new conditions, calm in the midst of chaos

3. **A.** Avoids conflict and drama, levelheaded
   B. Fun to be around, a good storyteller with a sense of humor
   C. Self-motivated, usually right
   D. Careful, thoughtful, doesn't rush into things

4. **A.** Upbeat, always sees the best in people and situations
   B. Detail-oriented, orderly, tidy
   C. Confident and assertive with my opinion
   D. Cooperative, open to the needs and ideas of others

5. **A.** A determined problem solver, finds a way to get it done
   B. Playful, spontaneous, lives in the moment
   C. Considerate, kind, polite
   D. Serious, avoids being impulsive or flashy

6. **A.** Friendly, outgoing, talkative
   B. Efficient and effective with my time and effort
   C. Relaxed, hard to provoke or annoy
   D. Precise, thorough, has very high standards

7. **A.** Not confident in social situations
   B. Can be quick-tempered
   C. Struggles to make decisions quickly
   D. Can dominate conversations

8. **A.** Unafraid to disagree with others, bossy
   B. Uncomfortable with solitude, afraid of missing out
   C. Rarely sets goals for myself, unclear on purpose or direction
   D. Sometimes feels isolated, too introspective

9. **A.** Can be overbearing, prefers to be in control
   B. Unsure of myself, reluctant to jump into conversations or activities
   C. Seeks diversions from tasks, can waste time or daydream
   D. Prone to feeling sad or gloomy, gets hung up on bad news

10. **A.** Persuades others to do things my way, thinks the end justifies the means ┈┈┈┈┈┈
    B. Often exaggerates stories, compulsive talker
    C. Uses sarcasm or the silent treatment when upset
    D. Struggles to express enthusiasm

11. **A.** No sense of urgency, resents being pushed
    B. Skeptical, sees obstacles, thinks about the worst-case scenario
    C. Fickle, forgetful, makes excuses, repeats stories
    D. Reluctant to admit mistakes or say I'm sorry, rarely compliments others

12. **A.** Struggles with follow-through, especially when things stop being fun
    B. Slow to get moving, a procrastinator
    C. Dislikes tears and emotions in others, can be unsympathetic
    D. Hard to please, can be critical

Choose the ONE statement that best represents you.

13. **A.** I like to talk through my decisions out loud with others.
    B. I am decisive and my decisions are usually right.
    C. I want all the information before I make a decision.
    D. I sometimes just want someone else to make the decision for me.

14. **A.** I like knowing a little about a lot of things and a lot about the things that really interest me.
    B. I like to stick to the schedule.
    C. I like accomplishing things and feeling productive.
    D. I like coming up with creative ideas people will enjoy.

15. **A.** I tend to notice imperfections and mistakes.
    B. I tend to forget or disregard things I'm not interested in.
    C. I tend to not even think of bad or sad things.
    D. I tend to not show my emotions.

16. **A.** I frequently tell stories about my personal experiences.
    B. I consider every thought and detail before communicating.
    C. I cut to the chase in conversations; I don't need every last detail.
    D. I hesitate to speak up and advocate for myself when I disagree with the group.

17. **A.** I want the freedom to do projects in my own time frame.
    B. I want time to process my thoughts and answers so I know they're correct.
    C. I want to know the why behind a project so I know it's worth my time.
    D. I want variety and spontaneity with projects.

18. **A.** I'm good at delegating to others.
    B. I'm good at teaching others.
    C. I'm good at inspiring others.
    D. I'm good at caring for others.

19. **A.** I get stressed when I feel like I'm not liked.
    B. I get stressed when I feel like I'm not understood.
    C. I get stressed when I feel like I'm not in control.
    D. I get stressed when I feel like I'm being pulled into conflict.

Choose the ONE phrase you are most likely to say in your head or out loud.

20. **A.** *Who else is going to be there?*
    B. *What will we be doing?*
    C. *Do I have to go?*
    D. *You go. I have better things to do.*

21. **A.** *Are you sure that's safe?*
    B. *Hurry up! We're late.*
    C. *That sounds like fun!*
    D. *I'm good with whatever.*

22. **A.** *It's done. I took care of it.*
    B. *I'll do it, if someone will do it with me.*
    C. *I've been giving it some thought.*
    D. *No worries, it will all work out.*

23. **A.** *No, thanks. I'll just watch.*
    B. *I didn't mean it that way.*
    C. *I'd be happy to help!*
    D. *I'm not sure I trust them.*

24. **A.** *I totally forgot about that. I'm sorry.*
    B. *I don't really care. You decide.*
    C. *That won't work. I've already planned to…*
    D. *Just give me the bottom line.*

Choose the ONE word/phrase of the four options that best describes you.
If you get stuck, just pick the best option available.

25. **A.** Easygoing
    B. Ambitious
    C. Energetic
    D. Analytical

26. **A.** Enthusiastic
    B. Fearless
    C. Agreeable
    D. Empathetic

27. **A.** Cautious
    B. Capable
    C. Calm
    D. Charming

28. **A.** Positive
    B. Organized
    C. Assertive
    D. Content

29. **A.** Resourceful
    B. Considerate
    C. Lighthearted
    D. Reserved

30. **A.** Productive
    B. Patient
    C. Detail-oriented
    D. People-oriented

31. **A.** Pessimistic
    B. Bossy
    C. Indifferent
    D. Distractible

32. **A.** Demanding
    B. Detached
    C. Naïve
    D. Moody

33. **A.** Self-centered
    B. Sluggish
    C. Scatterbrained
    D. Suspicious

34. **A.** Undisciplined
    B. Unmotivated
    C. Unsympathetic
    D. Unforgiving

35. **A.** Indecisive
    B. Dramatic
    C. Impatient
    D. Insecure

36. **A.** Blunt
    B. Judgmental
    C. Apathetic
    D. Restless

37. **A.** Driven
    B. Imaginative
    C. Compassionate
    D. Even-keeled

38. **A.** Well-balanced
    B. Enjoys working hard
    C. Musical or artistic
    D. Turns crisis into comedy

39. **A.** Methodical
    B. Loud laugh
    C. Quiet but witty
    D. Brave

40. **A.** Patient leader
    B. Curious
    C. Delegates well
    D. Deep and thoughtful

Turn the page to score your assessment.

DIRECTIONS FOR SCORING

1 ▶ Using the answer you wrote in the box, circle the corresponding letter in the scoring grid.

Circle the letter you wrote.   *Your answer*

1.	(D)	A	C	B	← 1.	*D*
2.	B	A	(C)	D	← 2.	*C*

2 ▶ Count the number of circles in each column to tally your score for each color.

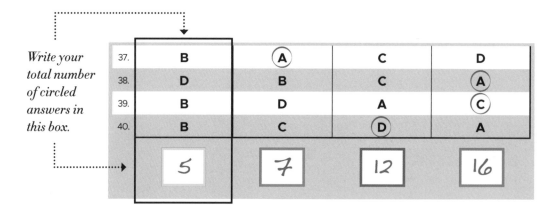

Write your total number of circled answers in this box.

37.	B	(A)	C	D
38.	D	B	C	(A)
39.	B	D	A	(C)
40.	B	C	(D)	A
	5	7	12	16

3 ▶ Turn the page to begin learning about your dominant temperament.

Double check!

Your scores in these four boxes should add up to 40.

#						#	Scoring		
1.	D	A	C	B	←	1.		B	A
2.	B	A	C	D	←	2.		C	C
3.	B	C	D	A	←	3.		BD	A
4.	A	C	B	D	←	4.		D	AB
5.	B	A	D	C	←	5.		C	D
6.	A	B	D	C	←	6.		D	B
7.	D	B	A	C	←	7.		C	C
8.	B	A	D	C	←	8.		D	D
9.	C	A	D	B	←	9.		B	B
10.	B	A	C	D	←	10.		D	C
11.	C	D	B	A	←	11.		A	B
12.	A	C	D	B	←	12.		A	D
13.	A	B	C	D	←	13.		C	B
14.	D	C	B	A	←	14.		A	A
15.	C	D	A	B	←	15.		B	D
16.	A	C	B	D	←	16.		D	B
17.	D	C	B	A	←	17.		B	A
18.	C	A	B	D	←	18.		D	B
19.	A	C	B	D	←	19.		D	D
20.	A	D	B	C	←	20.		B	B
21.	C	B	A	D	←	21.		B	B
22.	B	A	C	D	←	22.		C	C
23.	C	B	D	A	←	23.		C	B
24.	A	D	C	B	←	24.		B	A
25.	C	B	D	A	←	25.		D	P
26.	A	B	D	C	←	26.		D	C
27.	D	B	A	C	←	27.		A	A
28.	A	C	B	D	←	28.		D	B
29.	C	A	D	B	←	29.		D	B
30.	D	A	C	B	←	30.		C	C
31.	D	B	A	C	←	31.		C	C
32.	C	A	D	B	←	32.		B	B
33.	C	A	D	B	←	33.		D	D
34.	A	C	D	B	←	34.		D	C
35.	B	C	D	A	←	35.		C	C
36.	D	A	B	C	←	36.		D	C
37.	B	A	C	D	←	37.		A	D
38.	D	B	C	A	←	38.		A	B
39.	B	D	A	C	←	39.		A	A
40.	B	C	D	A	←	40.		D	B

Totals [ ] + [ ] + [ ] + [ ] = 40

2   4   9   3   17   16   13   17

UNDERSTANDING YOUR RESULTS

Once you've calculated your scores, typically two temperaments (colors) will stand out.

- The highest score is your dominant temperament.
- The second highest score is your secondary temperament.

We'll be focusing mostly on your dominant temperament throughout this study. Look back at your results on the previous page, and write in your numbers in the colored boxes below.

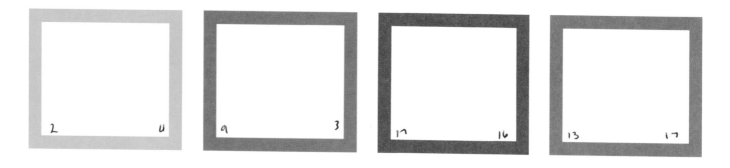

| 2 | 4 | 9 | 3 | 17 | 16 | 13 | 17 |

MY DOMINANT TEMPERAMENT IS...

Check One

☑ **SANGUINE/YELLOW**
I speak the language of people and fun.

☐ **CHOLERIC/RED**
I speak the language of power and control.

☐ **MELANCHOLIC/BLUE**
I speak the language of order and perfection.

☐ **PHLEGMATIC/GREEN**
I speak the language of calm and harmony.

COMMON RESULTS

Most commonly, your scores will result in dominant and secondary temperaments that are adjacent to (not diagonal from) one another on the quadrant. (Diagonal temperaments have almost opposite traits, so those combinations are unusual.)

✓ Dominant Choleric, Secondary Melancholic
✓ Dominant Sanguine, Secondary Phlegmatic
✗ Dominant Phlegmatic, Secondary Choleric

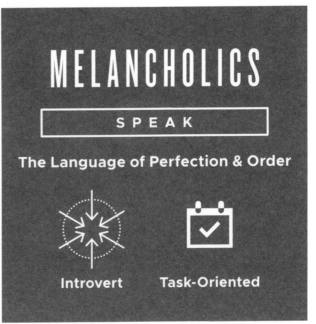

INTROVERTS & EXTROVERTS

Two of the four temperaments are considered introverts and the other two are extroverts (though there's often some confusion around what those terms really mean).

Introverts direct their thoughts and feelings **inward**.

Extroverts direct their thoughts and feelings **outward**.

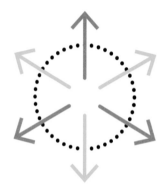

Introverts process their thoughts and feelings **before speaking**.

Extroverts process their thoughts and feelings **by speaking.**

TASK-ORIENTED & PEOPLE-ORIENTED

Two of the four temperaments are considered task-oriented and the other two are people-oriented.

Task-oriented people are inclined toward **accomplishing things**.

People-oriented people are inclined toward **fostering relationships**.

COMMON ASSESSMENT QUESTIONS

1. **What if my dominant and secondary temperaments are diagonal from each other?**

   Although assessment scores do occasionally result in these combinations, diagonal temperaments are not natural. For now, just focus on your dominant temperament (i.e., your highest score). Over the next few sessions, you may find yourself relating to a different secondary temperament. It's also possible that another dynamic—"masking"—is at play. (See the answer to question number four.)

2. **What if my two highest scores are the same or very close?**

   It's not unusual for scores to be very close or even exactly the same for your dominant and secondary temperaments. Over the next few sessions, pay attention to both. You may find that you identify more with one. That's likely your dominant temperament. If you can relate to both temperaments as you learn more about them, that's fine too. Think of yourself as "bilingual," able to speak the language of two temperaments. Since the goal of this study is to learn how to speak the language of all four temperaments, you have a head start!

3. **What if I only have _one_ high score (e.g., 20 or above)?**

   You have a particularly dominant temperament. Don't worry, this isn't a problem. In fact, it could make this study extra impactful for you. Our goal is to learn to speak the language of all four temperaments, and since only one comes naturally to you right now, you have an especially big opportunity.

4. **What if I have _three_ scores that are very close?**

   Learned behavior may appear in your results as a third temperament. We call this "masking." Your temperament is innate; it's what comes naturally to you. But you may have learned to mask your temperament in response to a person or circumstance.

   Typically (in up to 80% of cases), masking occurs as a response to parenting. In other words, you adjust your outward behavior to meet the standards or expectations imposed by a parent. Over time, it can be hard to distinguish this learned behavior from what comes naturally to you.

   Masking may also be a result of grief, trauma, or other abuse. These difficult circumstances may cause you to adopt behaviors for which you are not otherwise wired in order to protect your mental or physical well-being.

   If you have three scores that are very close, masking is a dynamic to be aware of and to hopefully process as you move through this study. But for now, focus on just your dominant temperament. To figure out which one that is, it may help to ask yourself: _What am I like when I'm by myself or in crisis?_

5. **What if I don't agree with my results?**

   That is perfectly normal. Consider chatting it over with a loved one or a close friend. They may be able to reflect back to you qualities that are tough to see in yourself. As you move forward in this study, you may find that results you disagree with now turn out to be more accurate than you think. (Of course, it's also possible that your results are in fact incorrect. It never hurts to double-check your scoring sheet.)

1-B	25-D
2-C	26-C
3-A	27-B
4-D	28-A
5-A	29-A
6-B	30-B
7-A	31-D
8-D	32-B
9-C	33-D
10-A	34-B
11	35-C
12-B	36-D
13-B	37-B
14-A	38-A
15-B	39-A
16-A	40-B
17-A	
18-B	
19-D	
20-B	
21-D	
22-C	
23-C	
24-B	

STRENGTHS & WEAKNESSES

STRENGTHS & WEAKNESSES

Session Two

STRENGTHS & WEAKNESSES

Session Two

Session Two at a Glance

During Session Two...

1 Review the last session's recap.

2 Watch the Session Two video (41 minutes).

3 Discuss the session questions.

Homework...

4 Read pages 51–54.

5 Complete the activities on pages 55–56.

You learned what language each of the four temperaments speaks and you completed the assessment to determine your dominant temperament.

▶ VIDEO NOTES

> Before you start watching the video, take a few minutes to share your assessment results with one another. What is your dominant temperament?

> CHECK OUT THE STRENGTHS AND WEAKNESSES LIST FOR EACH TEMPERAMENT ON THE FOLLOWING PAGES.

SANGUINE

Strengths	Weaknesses
1. Lives in the moment	1. Compulsive talker
2. Shows emotions openly	2. Exaggerates and elaborates
3. Inspiring	3. Dwells on trivial things
4. Great storyteller	4. Can't remember names
5. Optimistic	5. Scares others off
6. Joyful	6. Too happy for some
7. Curious	7. Has restless energy
8. Cheerful	8. Egotistical
9. Sincere	9. Blusters and complains
10. Popular	10. Naïve
11. Encouraging	11. Has loud voice and laugh
12. Persuasive	12. Controlled by circumstances
13. Creative	13. Gets angry easily
14. Volunteers for jobs	14. Seems phony to some
15. Active	15. Never grows up
16. People-oriented	16. Forgets obligations
17. Spontaneous	17. Doesn't follow through
18. Apologizes quickly	18. Confidence fades fast
19. Doesn't hold grudges	19. Undisciplined
20. Likes variety	20. Priorities out of order
21. Emotional, expressive, animated	21. Decides by feelings
22. Adventurous	22. Easily distracted
23. Affectionate	23. Hates to be alone
24. Accepts others easily	24. Wants to be popular
25. Can turn crisis into comedy	25. Looks for credit
26. Thinks quickly	26. Dominates conversations
27. Easy to talk to	27. Interrupts
28. Can express self directly in conflict	28. Answers for others
29. Works better with people	29. Makes excuses
30. Disciplined if tasks are fun/challenging	30. Repeats stories
31. Excellent at short-term projects	31. Doesn't listen
32. Excels when there are visible results	32. Hides insecurities
33. Non-judgmental	33. Self-centered
34. Good on stage	34. Impulsive
35. Inspires others to join	35. Vain
36. Has energy and enthusiasm	36. Disorganized
37. Looks great on the surface	37. Uncommitted
38. Charms others to work	38. Dramatic
39. Thrives on compliments	39. Scatterbrained
40. Charismatic	40. Showoff

CHOLERIC

Strengths	Weaknesses
1. Dynamic leader	1. Bossy
2. Delegates well	2. Impatient
3. Ability to correct wrongs	3. Quick-tempered
4. Decisive	4. Can't relax
5. Can control emotions in emergencies	5. Doesn't shy from controversy
6. Independent and self-sufficient	6. Enjoys arguments
7. Energetic	7. Won't give up when losing
8. Adventurous	8. Comes on too strong
9. Appears confident	9. Inflexible
10. Energized by challenges	10. Is not complimentary
11. Persuasive	11. Dislikes tears and emotions
12. Bold	12. Is unsympathetic
13. Resourceful, pragmatic	13. Little tolerance for mistakes
14. Self-directed	14. Doesn't analyze details
15. Disciplined	15. Bored by trivial things
16. Competitive	16. May make rash decisions
17. Not easily discouraged	17. May be rude or tactless
18. Leads and encourages production	18. Manipulates people
19. Practical	19. Demanding of others
20. Productive	20. End justifies the means
21. Moves quickly to action	21. Work may become an idol
22. Can take charge when needed	22. Demands loyalty
23. Is usually right	23. May use people
24. Efficient and effective with materials and time	24. Dominates
25. Gets it done	25. Knows everything
26. Authoritative and powerful	26. Can do everything better
27. Driven	27. Too independent
28. Influential	28. Possessive of friends or mate
29. Logical	29. Has trouble saying "I'm sorry"
30. Thrives on opposition	30. May be right, but unpopular
31. Committed and loyal	31. Decides for others
32. Articulates thoughts and ideas well	32. Headstrong
33. Great sense of perspective	33. Prideful
34. Responsible	34. Domineering
35. Comfortable with power	35. Intolerant
36. Capable of bouncing back from difficulties	36. Nervy
37. Always has a plan and a purpose	37. Selfish
38. Highly task-oriented	38. Arrogant
39. Compulsive need for change	39. Aggressive
40. Sets and achieves goals	40. Doesn't listen

PHLEGMATIC

Strengths	Weaknesses
1. Kind, considerate	1. Unenthusiastic
2. Balanced	2. Fearful
3. Accommodating	3. Worried
4. Easygoing and relaxed	4. Indecisive
5. Consistent	5. Avoids responsibility
6. Quiet but witty	6. Selfish
7. Listens well	7. Too shy
8. Diplomatic	8. Too compromising
9. Steady, even-tempered	9. Self-righteous
10. Friendly	10. Lacks self-motivation
11. Cooperative	11. Hard to get moving
12. Agreeable	12. Resents being pushed
13. Good under pressure	13. Can appear lazy
14. Mediator, negotiator	14. Discourages others
15. Reliable	15. Would rather watch
16. Content	16. No sense of urgency
17. Likeable	17. Dampens enthusiasm
18. Responsible	18. Stays uninvolved
19. Leader (shepherd)	19. Indifferent to plans
20. Faithful	20. Judges others
21. Compassionate	21. Sarcastic
22. Patient	22. Resists change
23. Can recognize all sides of issues	23. Doubtful
24. Receptive to ideas	24. Reticent
25. Does well when goals are clear	25. Teasing
26. Supportive	26. Messy
27. Tolerant	27. Timid
28. Appreciates strengths in others	28. Compromising
29. Great team player	29. Sluggish
30. Forgiving	30. Uninvolved
31. Generous	31. Ambivalent
32. Warm and inviting	32. Nonchalant
33. Cautious	33. Plain
34. Can work well alone	34. Aimless
35. Fair and tactful	35. Stubborn
36. Finds the easy way	36. Unexpressive
37. Sensible	37. Boring
38. Reflective	38. Mumbles
39. Not easily provoked or insulted	39. Hesitant
40. Great common sense	40. Blank

MELANCHOLIC

Strengths	Weaknesses
1. Empathetic	1. Remembers the negatives
2. Deep and thoughtful	2. Moody
3. Analytical	3. Enjoys being hurt
4. Serious and purposeful	4. Has false humility
5. Conscientious	5. Off in another world
6. Honest	6. Low self-image
7. Creative	7. Has selective hearing
8. Musical, artistic	8. Reserved
9. Works well alone	9. Too introspective
10. Great listener	10. Feelings of guilt
11. Orderly	11. Tends toward hypochondria
12. Emotionally secure	12. Not people-oriented
13. Philosophical and poetic	13. Depressed over imperfections
14. Idealistic	14. Hesitant to start projects
15. Excels in research	15. Spends too much time planning
16. High integrity	16. Prefers analysis to work
17. Perfectionist	17. Self-deprecating
18. Sensitive to others	18. Hard to please
19. Cautious	19. Standards often too high
20. Respectful	20. Insecure socially
21. Focused	21. Withdrawn and remote
22. Needs to finish what is started	22. Critical of others
23. Scheduled	23. Holds back affection
24. Detailed and accurate	24. Dislikes those in opposition
25. Neat, tidy	25. Suspicious
26. Sees the obstacles and finds creative solutions	26. Antagonistic
27. Sincere	27. Skeptical
28. Loyal and devoted	28. Revengeful
29. Makes charts, graphs, lists	29. Fearful
30. Problem solver	30. Unforgiving
31. Punctual	31. Judgmental
32. Enjoys solitude	32. Guarded
33. Deep friendships, quality over quantity	33. Self-righteous
34. Reflective	34. Worried
35. Can handle crisis with grace	35. Suspicious
36. Prefers facts and logic	36. Depressed
37. Self-sacrificing	37. Sensitive
38. Content to stay in the background	38. Hates to be interrupted
39. Moved to tears with compassion	39. Insecure
40. Methodical	40. Fears failure

DISCUSSION QUESTIONS

Because of the length of this session's video segment, it's perfectly fine if you don't have time to discuss all of these questions. Choose your favorites or consider saving the activity in question 3 to complete on your own.

1 ▶ Could you relate to the person in the video who shares your dominant temperament? Why or why not?

2 ▶ Kathleen defined an introvert as someone whose thoughts and feelings are directed inward (i.e., they think before they speak) and an extrovert as someone whose thoughts and feelings are directed outward (i.e., they speak before they think). Do those definitions change how you may have previously labeled yourself? Explain.

3 ▶ Take a few minutes to individually complete the *My Strengths & Weaknesses* activity on page 49. When you're finished, discuss the following questions as a group:

- Which strength of your temperament can you identify with?
- Which weakness of your temperament can you identify with?

4 ▶ Paul begins Ephesians 4:29 by saying, *"Do not let any unwholesome talk come out of your mouths."*

Take a look at the list of your weaknesses. Talk about a time one of your weaknesses caused you to hurt someone with your words.

5 ▶ In Ephesians 2:10, Paul writes, *"For we are God's handiwork, created in Christ Jesus to do good works, which God prepared in advance for us to do."*

How does the idea that God wired you on purpose for a purpose land with you?

HOMEWORK

▶ Read pages 51–54.

▶ Complete the activities on pages 55–56.

"MY STRENGTHS & WEAKNESSES" ACTIVITY

Refer to the lists of strengths and weaknesses for each temperament found on pages 44–47 to complete this activity.

▶ Read the list of strengths for your dominant temperament.

▶ Write down five (or more) strengths you recognize in yourself.

Reflective	Problem Solver
Work well alone	Thoughtful
Team Player	Sincere
work well / Goals are clear	Conscientious

▶ Read the list of weaknesses for your dominant temperament.

▶ Write down five (or more) weaknesses you recognize in yourself.

Indecisive	
Resent being pushed	
Skeptical	
Remembers the negative	

DO NOT LET ANY UNWHOLESOME TALK COME OUT OF YOUR MOUTHS,

but only what is helpful for building others up according to their needs, that it may benefit those who listen.

Ephesians 4:29

▶ SESSION READING

Our intentions are usually good. When given the choice between helping and hurting someone with our words, most of us most of the time would choose to help.

And yet . . .

We've all argued, ignored, or interrupted. We've given unwelcome advice or untrue excuses. We've yelled insults or whispered rumors. In short, we've let "unwholesome talk" come right out of our mouths.

Why? We're wired for it.

Each temperament has unique strengths and weaknesses. Your strengths are the very best version of you. You are wired perfectly for the purpose God has for you. Those strengths have a counterpoint, though. You are also wired with weaknesses that have the potential to ruin relationships and derail your life.

If that seems scary, here's some good news: you can *choose* to speak from your strengths or from your weaknesses. Until now, it probably hasn't felt that way—hurtful words have popped out of your mouth before you could hear them coming. But learning how you're wired will change that. Let me show you how.

Continued on the next page.

OVERVIEW OF THE FOUR TEMPERAMENTS

Here's a glance at the defining characteristics and one unique quality of each temperament.

SANGUINES

Loud strengths	Loud weaknesses	
Magnetic, inspiring, encouraging	Can elaborate and exaggerate, speak too loudly, and interrupt others	Uniquely wired to see the best in people and circumstances
Great storytellers who bring joy, laughter, and optimism to everything they do	Have a tendency to be forgetful and naïve	

CHOLERICS

Powerful strengths	Powerful weaknesses	
Responsible, decisive, and good at delegating	Can argue, dominate, and use a harsh tone	Uniquely wired to be visionaries who can see and achieve goals
Dynamic leaders who excel at managing tasks and projects	Have a tendency to be bossy, impatient, and intolerant	

MELANCHOLICS

Deep strengths	Deep weaknesses	
Both analytical and creative	Can remember the negatives, fear failure, and have low self-esteem	Uniquely wired to anticipate obstacles and creatively problem-solve
Perfectionists who are detailed, orderly, compassionate, and often artistic and/or musical	Have a tendency to be judgmental and critical	

PHLEGMATICS

Peaceful strengths	Peaceful weaknesses	
Easygoing, steady, calm, and patient	Can respond to stress by being slow and stubborn	Uniquely wired to stay calm and kind in the midst of chaos
Loyal friends and good listeners who excel at leading people	Have a tendency to avoid conflict, disengage, or be too compromising	

WHAT YOUR STRENGTHS & WEAKNESSES SOUND LIKE

If someone recorded you for a week, these are some of the things you would be likely to say:

In their strengths, they commonly say...

Oh, I've got a story about that... wait 'til you hear this!

That sounds fun!

In their weaknesses, they commonly say...

Do you always have to be so serious?

Oops! I completely forgot.

 SANGUINES

In their strengths, they commonly say...

How about we do it this way?

Can you get that finished for me today?

In their weaknesses, they commonly say...

Just do what I said.

Hurry up!

 CHOLERICS

In their strengths, they commonly say...

I'm good with whatever.

I think we can make that work.

In their weaknesses, they commonly say...

I'll do it later.

I don't know.

 PHLEGMATICS

In their strengths, they commonly say...

I've been giving it some thought...

I'm almost finished. I just want to fix one thing.

In their weaknesses, they commonly say...

No one understands me.

I'm worried about that.

 MELANCHOLICS

WHAT EACH TEMPERAMENT WANTS YOU TO KNOW

Each temperament's weaknesses may cause others to make incorrect assumptions about them. Here's what each temperament wishes we *really* understood about how they're wired.

 Sanguine: I want you to know that I'm intelligent and capable of being serious when it's required.

 Choleric: I want you to know that I've thought through my decisions and have good reasons for them.

 Melancholic: I want you to know that I'm reserved, but I really do want to be invited and included.

 Phlegmatic: I want you to know that I have ideas and opinions. If I don't speak up, please ask.

A Word of Warning

Anytime you describe or label entire categories of people, it's easy to lose the nuance. We see cholerics described as dynamic leaders, so we assume anyone in leadership or authority must be choleric. Or we see sanguines described as fun, so we assume everyone who has a sense of humor must be sanguine.

The similarities and differences between each temperament (especially opposite temperaments) can be subtle, but they're important to understand if we want to avoid incorrectly labeling others. Yes, cholerics are great leaders of projects, but phlegmatics are gifted leaders of people. Yes, sanguines are fun, but melancholics' unique point of view often makes them very funny.

When considering strengths and weaknesses, remember that opposite temperaments often have subtle twists of similar traits.

Pause and Choose

So how does all this labeling and describing help you avoid the "unwholesome talk" the apostle Paul warns against? How do lists of strengths and weaknesses help with your words?

You can now pause and choose.

Being aware of how you're wired allows you to stop and choose to respond from your strengths rather than blurting out a reply from your weaknesses. Here's the script for initiating the pause.

> ## I HAVE A TENDENCY TO (BE) _____,
> ## BUT I WILL CHOOSE TO (BE) _____.

It really is that simple. Easy? Well, not always. But next time we'll look at how we can more consistently speak from our strengths. It's not a matter of good days, bad days, or moods. Getting a grip on the words we say starts with the words we hear. More on that in the next session.

HOMEWORK ACTIVITIES

Ask Around

▶ Show the list of strengths and weaknesses for your temperament (from pages 44–47) to a trusted friend, spouse, parent, or sibling and ask them to write down five strengths and five weaknesses they see in you.

Strengths	Weaknesses
_____	_____
_____	_____
_____	_____
_____	_____
_____	_____
_____	_____

▶ Did anything your loved one reflected back to you come as a surprise? Take some notes here.

_____

_____

_____

HOMEWORK ACTIVITIES, CONTINUED

Pause and Choose

Let's come up with a script you can repeat when you hear yourself using the "unwholesome talk" of your weaknesses.

▶ Choose a weakness that comes naturally to you to complete the sentence:
I have a tendency to (be) _____.

▶ Then complete the sentence: *But I will choose to (be) _____.*

Examples:
I have a tendency to **interrupt**, but I will choose to be a **good listener**.
I have a tendency to be **bossy**, but I will choose to **delegate well**.
I have a tendency to **avoid responsibility**, but I will choose to be **cooperative**.
I have a tendency to be **critical**, but I will choose to be **compassionate**.

I HAVE A TENDENCY TO (BE) *recent being*

pushed ,

BUT I WILL CHOOSE TO (BE) *thoughtful*

& Constructive .

THE WORDS YOUR TEMPERAMENT NEEDS

NEEDS

Session Three

THE WORDS YOUR TEMPERAMENT NEEDS

Session Three at a Glance

During Session Three...

1 Review the last session's recap.

2 Watch the Session Three video (28 minutes).

3 Discuss the session questions.

Homework...

4 Read pages 65–68.

5 Complete the activities on pages 69–71.

IN THE LAST SESSION...

You learned the strengths and weaknesses of each temperament.

SANGUINES	**Loud strengths**	**Loud weaknesses**
	Magnetic, inspiring, encouraging	Elaborate and exaggerate, speak too loudly, and interrupt others
	Great storytellers who bring joy, laughter, and optimism to everything they do	Have a tendency to be forgetful and naïve

CHOLERICS	**Powerful strengths**	**Powerful weaknesses**
	Responsible, decisive, and good at delegating	Argue, dominate, and use a harsh tone
	Dynamic leaders who excel at managing tasks and projects	Have a tendency to be bossy, impatient, and intolerant

MELANCHOLICS	**Deep strengths**	**Deep weaknesses**
	Both analytical and creative	Remember the negatives, fear failure, and have low self-esteem
	Perfectionists who are detailed, orderly, compassionate, and often artistic and/or musical	Have a tendency to be judgmental and critical

PHLEGMATICS	**Peaceful strengths**	**Peaceful weaknesses**
	Easygoing, steady, calm, and patient	Respond to stress by being slow and stubborn
	Loyal friends and good listeners who excel at leading people	Have a tendency to avoid conflict, disengage, or be too compromising

VIDEO NOTES

_____

_____

_____

_____

_____

_____

_____

_____

_____

_____

_____

_____

_____

_____

_____

_____

_____

_____

_____

_____

_____

SANGUINES

INNATE NEEDS

Approval

Acceptance

Attention

Affection

CHOLERICS

INNATE NEEDS

Loyalty

Sense of Control

Appreciation

Credit for Work

PHLEGMATICS

INNATE NEEDS

Harmony

Feeling of Worth

Lack of Stress

Respect

MELANCHOLICS

INNATE NEEDS

Safety

Sensitivity

Support

Space & Silence

DISCUSSION QUESTIONS

1 ▶ What's your reaction to the four innate needs of your temperament?

2 ▶ Could you relate to any of the examples or stories you heard in the video? What resonated with you?

3 ▶ Take a few minutes to complete the *Full or Empty?* activity on pages 61–62. When you're finished, discuss the following questions as a group:

- Did any of your gauges surprise you? If so, which one(s)?
- Did the definitions/statements change the way you feel about any of your needs? If so, how?

4 ▶ In the video, Terrence shared a story about his wife filling his need for loyalty with her words. What has someone said that filled one of your needs? (Or, as he phrased it, "put wind in your sail.")

5 ▶ Now that you know your innate needs, what insights do you have into why certain words have been so impactful for you?

6 ▶ What message does culture send about your temperament's innate needs?

HOMEWORK

▶ Read pages 65–68.

▶ Complete the activities on pages 69–71.

"FULL OR EMPTY?" ACTIVITY

Take a few moments to gauge how full or empty your innate needs are right now. Find and mark the four scales for your dominant temperament. *(You can ignore the gauges for the other three temperaments.)*

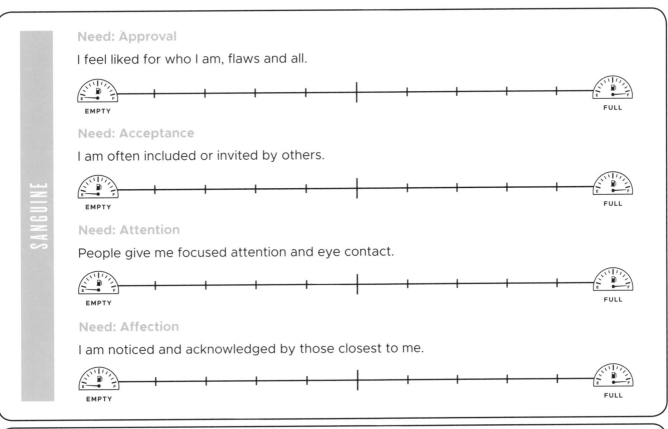

SANGUINE

Need: Approval

I feel liked for who I am, flaws and all.

EMPTY — FULL

Need: Acceptance

I am often included or invited by others.

EMPTY — FULL

Need: Attention

People give me focused attention and eye contact.

EMPTY — FULL

Need: Affection

I am noticed and acknowledged by those closest to me.

EMPTY — FULL

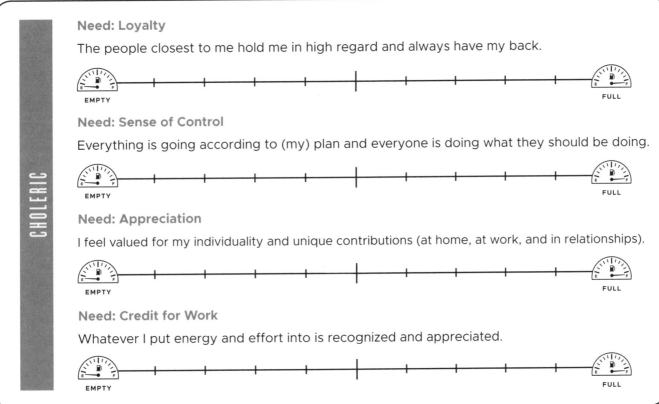

CHOLERIC

Need: Loyalty

The people closest to me hold me in high regard and always have my back.

EMPTY — FULL

Need: Sense of Control

Everything is going according to (my) plan and everyone is doing what they should be doing.

EMPTY — FULL

Need: Appreciation

I feel valued for my individuality and unique contributions (at home, at work, and in relationships).

EMPTY — FULL

Need: Credit for Work

Whatever I put energy and effort into is recognized and appreciated.

EMPTY — FULL

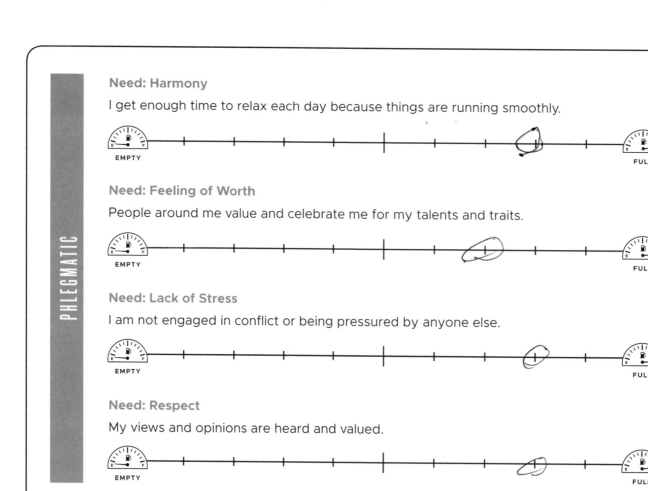

PHLEGMATIC

Need: Harmony

I get enough time to relax each day because things are running smoothly.

EMPTY — FULL

Need: Feeling of Worth

People around me value and celebrate me for my talents and traits.

EMPTY — FULL

Need: Lack of Stress

I am not engaged in conflict or being pressured by anyone else.

EMPTY — FULL

Need: Respect

My views and opinions are heard and valued.

EMPTY — FULL

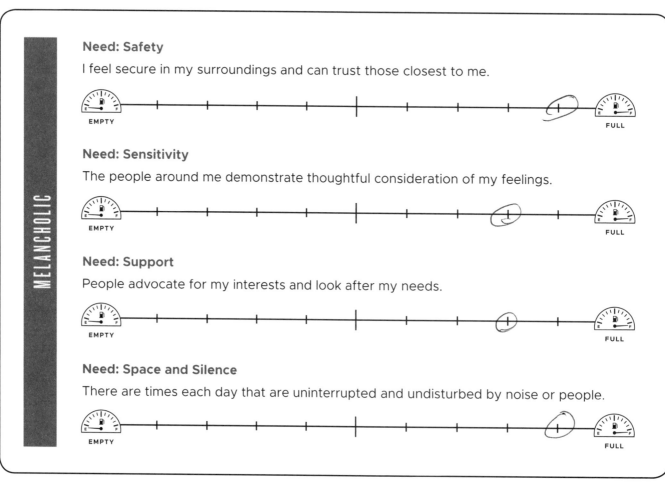

MELANCHOLIC

Need: Safety

I feel secure in my surroundings and can trust those closest to me.

EMPTY — FULL

Need: Sensitivity

The people around me demonstrate thoughtful consideration of my feelings.

EMPTY — FULL

Need: Support

People advocate for my interests and look after my needs.

EMPTY — FULL

Need: Space and Silence

There are times each day that are uninterrupted and undisturbed by noise or people.

EMPTY — FULL

Do not let any
unwholesome talk come
out of your mouths, but
only what is helpful
for building others up

ACCORDING TO
THEIR NEEDS,

that it may benefit
those who listen.

Ephesians 4:29

SESSION READING

Words don't carry equal weight for everyone. A comment that one person brushes off may leave another devastated. What motivates one may overwhelm another. What you forget, I may remember for years. This is one of the things that makes communication so challenging.

The next piece of the temperaments framework helps us make some sense of it, though.

Each temperament has a set of innate needs that are filled through words that others say to us and words we say to ourselves.

SANGUINES
INNATE NEEDS

Approval

Acceptance

Attention

Affection

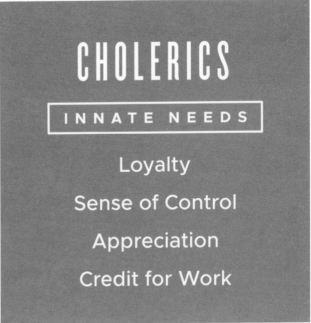

CHOLERICS
INNATE NEEDS

Loyalty

Sense of Control

Appreciation

Credit for Work

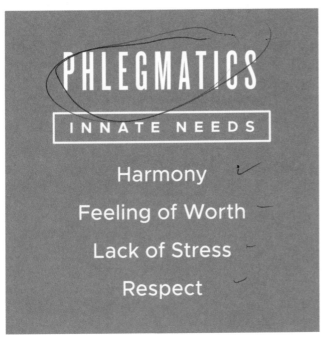

PHLEGMATICS
INNATE NEEDS

Harmony

Feeling of Worth

Lack of Stress

Respect

MELANCHOLICS
INNATE NEEDS

Safety

Sensitivity

Support

Space & Silence

These innate needs explain why words land differently for each of us. A comment like, "You should come!" may feel stressful for a melancholic who needs space and silence, but it probably energizes a sanguine who is wired to need acceptance.

This is the dynamic the apostle Paul underscores when he urges us to choose our words "according to *their* needs." We should consider how our words will feel to the person we're talking to. It's not safe to assume that they will react the same way we would. Choosing to use words the other person is wired for is a way to ensure we're building them up, not tearing them down in every conversation.

PUTTING IT INTO WORDS

Because we're wired differently, it can be hard to understand the needs of other temperaments. In fact, it can be hard to understand the needs of *your* temperament! A concept like "respect" could mean something different to you than me, even if we're both phlegmatic. So let's get a high-level view of what each of the innate needs may sound or look like in our everyday lives.

	Need...	Which sounds or looks like...	
SANGUINES	Approval	Being liked for who they are, without needing to change	"Come! It's always better when you're there."
	Acceptance	Being invited and included	
	Attention	Having your full focus, especially eye contact	
	Affection	Being noticed or acknowledged	
CHOLERICS	Loyalty	Being prioritized, knowing you had their back	"Wow! You put a lot of time and effort into this."
	Sense of Control	Everyone pulling their weight, following the plan	
	Appreciation	Being valued for their unique strengths	
	Credit for Work	Being valued for their contributions	
MELANCHOLICS	Safety	Being able to trust their surroundings and relationships	"You have a lot on your plate right now, so I took care of this for you."
	Sensitivity	Being understood	
	Support	Being offered or provided help	
	Space & Silence	Having time to decompress, process, or think	
PHLEGMATICS	Harmony	Everyone getting along or everything going smoothly	"You always have a great perspective. I'd love to hear your thoughts."
	Feeling of Worth	Being valued for their unique strengths	
	Lack of Stress	An absence of conflict and combative words	
	Respect	Being asked for their thoughts or opinions	

You May Have Noticed...

The innate needs of each temperament complement the language of that temperament. For example, sanguines speak the language of fun and people. So it's not a surprise that their four needs are related to fun and people. Cholerics speak the language of power and control. It makes sense that they crave words that celebrate how powerful and productive they are.

Finding Freedom

Culture sends mixed messages about many of the innate needs. We're told that needing control makes us bossy or that needing sensitivity makes us weak. As a result, most of us have been saddled with some degree of confusion around these needs—often going all the way back to childhood. It's easy to see how a sanguine kid's need for attention could get him labeled as hyperactive or how a phlegmatic child's need to avoid stress could make him look lazy.

Hopefully, learning that God wired you with these needs helps clear up some of your confusion. Not only is it *okay* for you to crave these things, it's *vital* that you get them! When you leverage your strengths to fill your needs, you are authentically the person God created you to be.

Why Are These Needs "Filled," Not "Met"?

Innate needs never go away. There is no amount of sensitivity that will ever completely meet a melancholic's need for sensitivity. There is no amount of harmony that will ever fully and finally satisfy a phlegmatic's need for harmony. We wake up every day with renewed appetites.

It's helpful to instead think of it as *filling* these needs. Just like eating food fills your appetite for a little while, hearing the words you crave fills your appetite for a little while. Eventually, though, you'll get "hungry" again.

Continued on the next page.

LOOKING INWARD AND UPWARD

We each have a community of people that can fill our needs with the words they speak to us—our spouses, kids, parents, friends, colleagues, and even perfect strangers. Ideally, the people closest to you are aware of your needs and actively try to accomplish Ephesians 4:29 by speaking "according to [your] needs."

But relying only on others to fill your innate needs will often leave you... empty. Maybe your spouse isn't interested, your family is distant, or your friends are distracted. What then?

Next session, we'll look at the ways we're wired to respond when our needs aren't filled, but let me jump ahead and assure you of two things.

1. **You play a part.** You are not at the mercy of other people's words to fill your needs. Each time you choose a strength over a weakness, you are giving yourself a dose of what you crave. When phlegmatics choose to be kind, they are creating the harmony they need. When melancholics choose to be empathetic, they are creating the sensitivity they need.

2. **God plays a part.** While you may not audibly hear God's voice, he is the ultimate source of the words you crave. Scripture captures Jesus' words; look to them when your needs are unfilled. And consider how you can structure your relationship with God in a way that fills your needs. For example, a choleric could keep a journal of answered prayers as a snapshot of God's loyalty. Or a sanguine could find acceptance by focusing on the truth that they have been adopted into God's family.

The words other people say to us are certainly an important source of what we're wired to need. Acknowledging this underscores the incredible impact we can have when we speak "according to their needs" in every conversation. We can be the source of the words others are so desperately craving. But if others are not equipped or able to do the same for us, we are not forsaken. We can choose to lean into our strengths and to lean into God.

HOMEWORK ACTIVITIES

How Do I Define It?

Even if two people have the same temperament, it's likely they'll describe each of their innate needs a little differently. Lofty concepts like "respect" and "loyalty" don't have a single definition. So let's spend some time thinking about what your personal definitions may be.

▶ Fill in your four innate needs below and try to define them in just a few words. Then come up with an example of something someone could say that will help fill that need for you.

The "Putting It Into Words" chart on page 66 has a high-level definition for each innate need. Refer back to it to jump-start your thoughts (if needed).

Example:
I need: Affection
Which I define as: Being desired or admired
So it would feel good if someone said: "You were the sharpest person at the party."

I need: Harmony

Which I define as: Things going smoothly, not chaotic, not agrumentative

So it would feel good if someone said: _____

I need: Feeling of Worth

Which I define as: Being valued — not

So it would feel good if someone said: Thanks for being around

I need: Lack of Stress

Which I define as: A Sense of Calm Settled situation (word)

So it would feel good if someone said: You're a Smoothing influence

I need: Respect

Which I define as: Listening to a variety of thoughts/opinions

So it would feel good if someone said: You listen to a lot of differing perspectives respectfully

HOMEWORK ACTIVITIES, CONTINUED

God Plays a Part

God is willing and able to fill your needs, and he can even do it with words! Here are some Scripture verses for each temperament that may be encouraging when you're craving words to fill a need.

▶ Read the Scripture verses for your dominant temperament.

▶ Consider memorizing one of the verses and/or displaying it somewhere as a reminder to lean into God to fill your innate needs.

INNATE NEED	SANGUINE BIBLE VERSES
Attention	Are not five sparrows sold for two pennies? Yet not one of them is forgotten by God. Indeed, the very hairs of your head are all numbered. Don't be afraid; you are worth more than many sparrows. (Luke 12:6–7)
Approval	Am I now trying to win the approval of human beings, or of God? Or am I trying to please people? If I were still trying to please people, I would not be a servant of Christ. (Galatians 1:10)
Acceptance	He chose us in him before the creation of the world to be holy and blameless in his sight. (Ephesians 1:4)
Affection	But you, Lord, are a compassionate and gracious God… abounding in love and faithfulness. (Psalm 86:15)

INNATE NEED	CHOLERIC BIBLE VERSES
Control	Commit to the Lord whatever you do, and he will establish your plans. (Proverbs 16:3)
Loyalty	Those who know your name trust in you, for you, Lord, have never forsaken those who seek you. (Psalm 9:10)
Credit for Work	Whatever you do, work at it with all your heart, as working for the Lord… since you know that you will receive an inheritance from the Lord as a reward. (Colossians 3:23–24)
Appreciation	For you [God] created my inmost being; you knit me together in my mother's womb. I praise you because I am fearfully and wonderfully made; your works are wonderful, I know that full well. (Psalm 139:13–14)

INNATE NEED	PHLEGMATIC BIBLE VERSES
Lack of Stress	Come to me, all you who are weary and burdened, and I will give you rest. (Matthew 11:28)
Respect	Make it your ambition to lead a quiet life: You should mind your own business and work with your hands... so that your daily life may win the respect of outsiders. (1 Thessalonians 4:11–12)
Feeling of Worth	But the Lord said to Samuel, "Do not consider his appearance or his height... The Lord does not look at the things people look at. People look at the outward appearance, but the Lord looks at the heart." (1 Samuel 16:7)
Harmony	Blessed are the peacemakers, for they will be called children of God. (Matthew 5:9)

INNATE NEED	MELANCHOLIC BIBLE VERSES
Support	[God] gives strength to the weary and increases the power of the weak. (Isaiah 40:29)
Safety	But the Lord is faithful, and he will strengthen you and protect you from the evil one. (2 Thessalonians 3:3)
Sensitivity	Therefore do not worry about tomorrow, for tomorrow will worry about itself. Each day has enough trouble of its own. (Matthew 6:34)
Space & Silence	The Lord is my shepherd... He makes me lie down in green pastures, he leads me beside quiet waters, he refreshes my soul. (Psalm 23:1–3)

WHEN YOUR NEEDS AREN'T FILLED

UNFILLED
NEEDS

UNFILLED
NEEDS

Session Four

WHEN YOUR NEEDS AREN'T FILLED

Session Four at a Glance

During Session Four...

1 Review the last session's recap.

2 Watch the Session Four video (16 minutes).

3 Discuss the session questions.

Homework...

4 Read pages 79–81.

5 Complete the activities on pages 82–83.

IN THE LAST SESSION...

You learned the innate needs of each temperament.

SANGUINES
INNATE NEEDS

Approval

Acceptance

Attention

Affection

CHOLERICS
INNATE NEEDS

Loyalty

Sense of Control

Appreciation

Credit for Work

PHLEGMATICS
INNATE NEEDS

Harmony

Feeling of Worth

Lack of Stress

Respect

MELANCHOLICS
INNATE NEEDS

Safety

Sensitivity

Support

Space & Silence

VIDEO NOTES

_____

_____

_____

_____

_____

_____

_____

_____

_____

_____

_____

_____

_____

_____

_____

_____

_____

_____

_____

SANGUINES

MANIPULATE WITH

Charm & Flattery

CHOLERICS

MANIPULATE WITH

Tone & Volume

PHLEGMATICS

MANIPULATE WITH

Procrastination & Stubbornness

MELANCHOLICS

MANIPULATE WITH

Moods & Silence

DISCUSSION QUESTIONS

1 ▶ What's your reaction to the word "manipulate"? What do you think of the idea that you manipulate others when your needs are unfilled? (If it helps, manipulate is defined as "to influence, especially in an unfair manner.")

2 ▶ Do you agree with the manipulating reaction of your temperament? (Turn back to the video notes page if you need a reminder.) Explain why or why not.

3 ▶ In the video, Kathleen posed the following scenarios:

SANGUINE	You and your spouse have plans to go to dinner with friends, but at the last minute your spouse doesn't want to go.
CHOLERIC	You're trying to get out the door on time with your kids, and they aren't moving fast enough.
MELANCHOLIC	After a tough week, you come home and are surprised to find a party happening at your house.
PHLEGMATIC	Someone nags you about a list of tasks you haven't completed yet. *or something doesn't work as it is supposed to (like sound system)*

How would you react to a similar scenario? Could you relate to the response of the person who shares your dominant temperament?

4 ▶ Can you recognize the manipulating reaction of someone else you interact with often (e.g., your spouse, child, boss, or colleague)? How has it impacted your relationship?

5 ▶ Can you think of a recent example when you may have (unknowingly) reacted to someone with manipulation? If you feel brave, share the story. If you'd rather skip the specifics, share an *aha* moment related to the way you've behaved in the past. *making comments about grandchildren or church*

6 ▶ When you feel like you're on the verge of speaking unwholesome, manipulating words, what can you do to change your response?

> *"Do not let any unwholesome talk come out of your mouths, but only what is helpful for building others up according to their needs that it may benefit those who listen."*

Ephesians 4:29

HOMEWORK

▶ Read pages 79–81.

▶ Complete the activities on pages 82–83.

DO NOT LET ANY UNWHOLESOME TALK COME OUT OF YOUR MOUTHS,

but only what is helpful
for building others
up according to their
needs, that it may benefit
those who listen.

Ephesians 4:29

SESSION READING

Best-case scenario: your loved ones consistently use exactly the words you're craving, so you get your innate needs filled, stay in your strengths, and are constantly the very best version of you.

That's not reality though, is it?

Of course not. Our innate needs will never be filled by everyone in every conversation. Melancholics will sometimes have trouble trusting. Phlegmatics will face conflict. Sanguines will be left out. Cholerics will be betrayed.

So what happens then?

Each temperament has a "tell"—a kind of subconscious reaction that occurs when our needs aren't filled. It shows up in our words (or, in some cases, in our lack of words). And it's used to manipulate others into giving us what we're craving.

SANGUINES
MANIPULATE WITH
Charm & Flattery

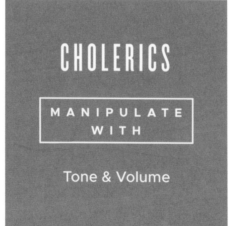

CHOLERICS
MANIPULATE WITH
Tone & Volume

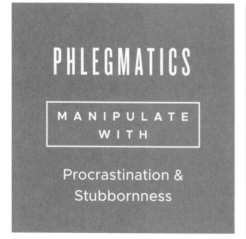

PHLEGMATICS
MANIPULATE WITH
Procrastination & Stubbornness

MELANCHOLICS
MANIPULATE WITH
Moods & Silence

These responses are some of the "unwholesome talk" the apostle Paul warns us to avoid in Ephesians 4:29. They may not seem unwholesome at first glance. (Melancholics may even argue that silence is saving them from using much more unwholesome language!) Consider the motive, though. When we use manipulating words, we are not thinking of the other person. We're selfishly prioritizing our own needs—the opposite of speaking "according to their needs" like Paul suggests.

PUTTING IT INTO WORDS

We slip into manipulating so naturally, we may not even notice we're doing it. So let's review what it may sound or look like for each temperament in our everyday lives.

	Manipulate with...	Which sounds or looks like...	
SANGUINES	Charm	Elaborating or exaggerating, being "over the top"	"You won't believe it... listen to this!"
	Flattery	Phony or excessive praise of others	
CHOLERICS	Tone	Harsh or biting comments	"I'll just do it myself."
	Volume	Angry outbursts, yelling	
MELANCHOLICS	Moods	Being judgmental, critical, or self-deprecating	"That will never work."
	Silence	Being disengaged, unwilling to talk to or hear from others	
PHLEGMATICS	Procrastination	Delaying or ignoring responsibilities	"Okay. I'll do it later."
	Stubbornness	Refusing to converse or compromise	

Silence

You May Have Noticed...

The way each temperament manipulates is an extreme version of the language of their temperament. For example, phlegmatics speak the language of calm. When their needs aren't filled, they push calm to the extreme by stubbornly refusing to take any action at all. Melancholics speak the language of perfection. When they don't get what they need, they respond with the extreme version—*perfect* silence. Sanguines speak the language of fun, which becomes reckless, exaggerated fun when their needs aren't filled. And cholerics speak the language of power, which they dial up using extreme volume.

The manipulating words of each temperament are, unfortunately, unhealthy displays of their temperament's weaknesses.

Heed the Warning

It's not particularly pleasant to admit to this part of your temperament. You may have lost a job, lost respect, or lost a relationship because of the way you reacted to someone. And you probably had no idea what was behind your angry outburst or foul mood.

Let's change that. You can prevent doing catastrophic damage if you use your manipulating words as a warning. Think of the dashboard light that lets you know your car is almost out of gas. Just like that light, your manipulating words warn you that your needs haven't been filled lately—you're "running on empty."

When you recognize that you're reacting with your temperament's manipulating words, stop and ask:

1. *What part do I play in this? What unfilled need is causing this reaction?*
2. *What could I have said or done differently?*

Instead of recklessly trying to fill your need out of your weaknesses, you can step into your strengths.

HOMEWORK ACTIVITIES

"So What Happened Was..."

Think about a time you responded with manipulating words. What were the circumstances? Knowing what you now know about your needs, which one of your four needs may not have been met in the moment?

▶ **So what happened was...** (Write out the details. Be honest.)

_____

_____

_____

_____

▶ **I manipulated with...** (Check one.)

☐ Charm	☐ Tone	☐ Moods	☐ Procrastination
☐ Flattery	☐ Volume	☐ Silence	☐ Stubbornness

▶ **Because I was needing... and wasn't getting it.** (Check one.)

☐ Approval	☐ Loyalty	☐ Safety	☒ Harmony
☐ Acceptance	☐ Sense of Control	☐ Sensitivity	☐ Worthiness
☐ Attention	☐ Appreciation	☐ Support	☐ Lack of Stress
☐ Affection	☐ Credit for Work	☐ Space & Silence	☐ Respect

▶ **My need for** _____ **could have been filled by...**
         (see above)

_____

_____

_____

Your Part + God's Part

Relying only on others to fill your needs will often leave you disappointed and vulnerable to reacting with manipulation.

▶ **Your Part:** What are some ways you can do your part to get what you're craving?

*Example: I am wired to need **loyalty**, which I could fill by **scheduling dinner out with friends**.*

I am wired to need _____,

which I could fill by _____.

I am wired to need _____,

which I could fill by _____.

▶ **God's Part:** We all connect with God differently (e.g., through nature, music, or serving others), and our temperaments may be a factor. Can you think of a way to structure your spiritual practices that would allow God to fill one of your innate needs?

*Example: I am wired to need **sensitivity**, which I could find from God by **journaling my thoughts/ prayers**.*

I am wired to need _____,

which I could find from God by _____.

IDENTIFYING OTHERS

IDENTIFYING OTHERS

Session Five

IDENTIFYING OTHERS

Session Five at a Glance

During Session Five...

1 Review the last session's recap.

2 Watch the Session Five video (35 minutes).

3 Discuss the session questions.

Homework...

4 Read pages 95–100.

5 Complete the activity on page 101.

IN THE LAST SESSION...

You learned how each temperament responds when their needs aren't filled.

SANGUINES

MANIPULATE WITH

Charm & Flattery

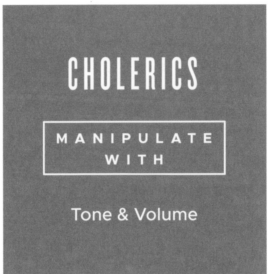

CHOLERICS

MANIPULATE WITH

Tone & Volume

PHLEGMATICS

MANIPULATE WITH

Procrastination &
Stubbornness

MELANCHOLICS

MANIPULATE WITH

Moods & Silence

VIDEO NOTES

DISCUSSION QUESTIONS

1 ▶ What stood out to you in the video? Could you relate to anything that was said?

2 ▶ Take a few minutes to complete the *Mapping Others* activity on page 93. When you're finished, discuss the following questions as a group:

- Who did you choose? Were you able to identify a possible temperament?
- How does thinking about their temperament help explain your past interactions or the dynamics of your relationship?

3 ▶ In the video, Terrence shared the story of his friend changing her approach to getting her daughter out of bed in the morning after identifying the daughter's phlegmatic temperament. Have you had any similar *aha* moments as you've thought about the temperaments of your loved ones? Share with the group.

4 ▶ In John 13:35, Jesus says, "By this everyone will know that you are my disciples, if you *love one another*." How does understanding the temperaments help you *love one another*?

5 ▶ Knowing about each temperament can change the way you hear and interpret other people's words. As Terrence said, "Knowing God wired them that way makes it easier to... give 'em a little bit of grace."

- Has this already been true for you? How?
- How does this change the way you think about and give *yourself* grace?

HOMEWORK

▶ Read pages 95–100.

▶ Complete the exercise on page 101.

"MAPPING OTHERS" ACTIVITY

Who are you curious about? Let's start narrowing down what their temperament may be by considering a few of their natural tendencies.

▶ **I am most curious to identify the temperament of:** _____ .

(Name)

▶ Introverts think before speaking. Extroverts speak before thinking. **They are...** (Check two.)

☐ Extroverted	☐ Extroverted	☐ Introverted	☐ Introverted

▶ Task-oriented people are energized by accomplishing things. People-oriented people are energized by connecting with others. **They are...** (Check two.)

☐ Task-Oriented	☐ People-Oriented	☐ Task-Oriented	☐ People-Oriented

▶ In a typical conversation, **what kind of words do they use?** (Check one.)

☐ Bold, confident	☐ Animated, optimistic	☐ Detailed, empathetic	☐ Calm, considerate

▶ When they're not getting their way, **how are they likely to react?** (Check one.)

☐ With volume	☐ With charm	☐ With moodiness	☐ With stubbornness

▶ **Count your check marks for each color and write the totals in the boxes below.** The color with the highest total may be their temperament.

Do not let any
unwholesome talk come
out of your mouths, but

ONLY WHAT
IS HELPFUL
FOR BUILDING
OTHERS UP

according to their needs,
that it may benefit
those who listen.

Ephesians 4:29

SESSION READING

So far, we've focused on understanding *your* wiring. What you've learned will help you fill your needs and stay in your strengths. That's how you'll accomplish the apostle Paul's first instruction in Ephesians 4:29 to "not let any unwholesome talk come out of your mouths."

To put it more simply, that's how you'll avoid tearing down others with your words. But how do you take it a step further and *build them up* with your words?

After all, Paul doesn't end his advice there. He continues by telling us to choose words that are "helpful for building others up." That means it's time to take what you've learned about yourself and the temperaments framework and apply it to others.

Perhaps you've already been trying to figure out the temperament of your spouse, child, boss, or best friend. That's great! Identifying someone's temperament is the first step toward choosing words that will build them up. So let's find out how we can reliably do it—even if our conversation is as brief as a trip through the checkout line.

Identifying Others

There are a few clues that can help you determine someone else's temperament (short of having them take the assessment). Depending on how well you know the person, some methods may be more helpful than others.

Remember that temperament is innate. Outward behavior may not always be an accurate indicator (e.g., just because someone likes the attention of performing on stage, they may not necessarily be sanguine). The most reliable way to determine someone's temperament is to figure out their core wiring. *What seems to come most naturally?*

Continued on the next page.

HERE ARE A FEW THINGS TO CONSIDER AS YOU TRY TO IDENTIFY SOMEONE ELSE'S TEMPERAMENT:

1. **What are they like on a good day?**

In Session 2, we learned that our temperament's strengths combine to make us *uniquely* good at something the other temperaments are not innately wired for.

Recognizing these strengths in someone is a foolproof way to identify their temperament. For example, if your child is an optimist who's always recapping her day with exclamations like, "It was so fun," she's most likely sanguine. If your spouse stays calm despite a mountain of disorder, he's probably phlegmatic.

These behaviors may not always be obvious, though. What then?

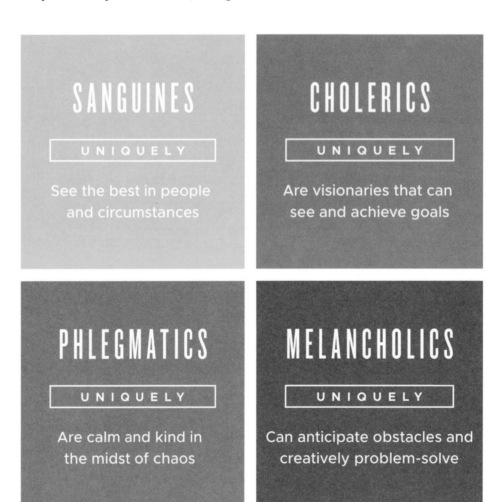

SANGUINES

UNIQUELY

See the best in people and circumstances

CHOLERICS

UNIQUELY

Are visionaries that can see and achieve goals

PHLEGMATICS

UNIQUELY

Are calm and kind in the midst of chaos

MELANCHOLICS

UNIQUELY

Can anticipate obstacles and creatively problem-solve

2. **What are they like on a tough day?**

Last session we learned that each temperament has a "tell"—a kind of subsconscious response we use when our needs aren't filled.

Just like strengths, these weaknesses also point to someone's temperament. You may not always know the need that isn't being filled at the moment, but hearing your boss escalate the volume every time a conversation gets heated may tell you she's choleric. Or noticing that your friend is quick to criticize when things aren't going his way may indicate he's melancholic.

Continued on the next page.

HERE ARE A FEW THINGS TO CONSIDER AS YOU TRY TO IDENTIFY SOMEONE ELSE'S TEMPERAMENT (CONTINUED):

3. **What language comes naturally to them?**

Everyday conversation can reveal the temperament of the person you're talking to. This is a particularly fun way to guess the temperament of someone you're only interacting with briefly, like a cashier or waiter. Simply listen for words that match the language of one of the four temperaments.

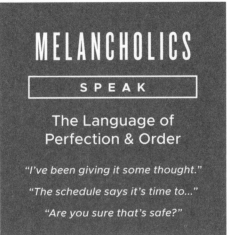

4. **What are their tendencies?**

Two of the four temperaments are introverts. The other two are extroverts.

- **Introverts** process their thoughts and feelings **before speaking**.
- **Extroverts** process their thoughts and feelings by **speaking**.

Similarly, two of the four temperaments are task-oriented, and the other two are people-oriented.

- **Task-oriented** people are inclined toward **accomplishing things**.
- **People-oriented** people are inclined toward **fostering relationships**.

Figuring out these tendencies in someone else can help you narrow down their possible temperament.

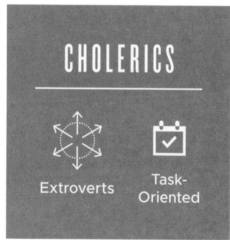

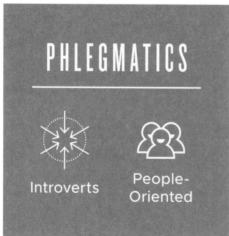

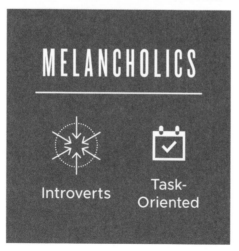

"It May Benefit Those Who Listen."

Once you know someone's temperament, you know the four things they are wired to need. So you can deliberately choose words they crave. For example, once you figure out your colleague is phlegmatic, you can fill his need for respect by specifically asking for his opinion in your next meeting. Or once you know your mom is choleric, you can fill her need for appreciation by saying something like, "I'm so lucky to have you."

Knowing the right words to say is a big upside of identifying someone's temperament. It's how you'll accomplish Paul's instruction to choose words that are "helpful for building others up."

It's not the only upside, though. Knowing someone's temperament also tells you the weaknesses and manipulating words they are wired for. You'll have the heads-up before you're on the receiving end of charm, tone, stubbornness, or silence on a tough day.

Knowing that these weaknesses are part of someone's wiring will give you more grace when they appear. Rather than taking hurtful interactions personally, you can view them as clues that the person has an unfilled need you may be able to speak into. When your sanguine brother starts dominating the conversation, you can respond gracefully, knowing that he needs affection. Maybe a comment like, "You always have the funniest stories," will help him get back on track.

The real impact of the temperaments framework is how it affects your relationships—specifically, how it expands your grace for others and equips you to use your words well. We're going to make it even more practical next session as we continue applying this framework to our interactions and conversations with others.

HOMEWORK ACTIVITY

Talk It Over

In Session 3, the *How Do I Define It?* homework (on page 69) helped you come up with a short, personal definition for each of your innate needs.

Understanding exactly what someone could say to fill your need for appreciation or support, for example, will make you more attuned to those words in your everyday life. But there's no sense in keeping it a secret! Telling someone which words are most meaningful to you increases the likelihood they'll use them.

If you haven't had a chance to complete the *How Do I Define It?* activity, turn to page 69 and give it a try now. It is tremendously helpful.

▶ **Here's your challenge: tell someone.** You could tell your spouse, best friend, or boss—anyone you interact with a lot. Use the *How Do I Define It?* activity as a guide, and share your definition for each innate need. If you can, mention an example of something they've said in the past that felt great.

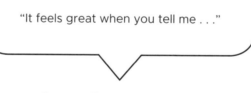

"It feels great when you tell me . . ."

▶ **Take notes.** Ask which words are meaningful to them and jot down how you can use those words in the future.

_____

_____

_____

_____

_____

PUTTING IT
INTO PRACTICE

PRACTICAL
TOOLS

PRACTICAL
TOOLS

Session Six

PUTTING IT INTO PRACTICE

During Session Six...

1 Discuss the Opening Question (page 106).

2 Watch the Session Six video (24 minutes).

3 Discuss the session questions.

OPENING QUESTION

Last session, you learned how to identify the temperament of others. **Whose temperament have you been able to identify since then? Share what you observed about or heard from that person that helped you figure it out.**

VIDEO NOTES

_____

_____

_____

_____

_____

_____

_____

_____

_____

_____

_____

_____

_____

YOUR ACTION PLAN

1 ▶ Stay in your strengths.
Use the Strength Training Tips on pages 111–113.

2 ▶ Work on your weaknesses.
Use the Scripture verses for your temperament on pages 115–117.

3 ▶ Be a builder.
Use the Build-Up Guide on pages 119–123.

DISCUSSION QUESTIONS

1 ▶ We've spent six sessions breaking down Ephesians 4:29.

Do not let any unwholesome talk come out of your mouths	Avoid hurtful words
but only what is helpful for building others up	Verbalize helpful words
according to their needs	Know which words fill their needs
that it may benefit those who listen.	Remember the power of your words

- Which portion of Ephesians 4:29 is hardest for you?
- What tools or insights do you now have that will help you improve in that area?

2 ▶ Take a few minutes to individually complete the *Action Plan* activity. When you're finished, discuss the following questions as a group:

- Who have you chosen to build up with your words?
- What action from the **Build-Up Guide** are you going to try in your next conversation with that person?

Bonus: How can the group encourage you to follow through?

3 ▶ What (if any) piece of the temperaments framework is still unclear for you? What are you unsure about or still stuck on?

 Kathleen may be able to help! Visit iSaidYouHeard.study/askKathleen to read her responses to commonly asked questions or to submit your own.

4 ▶ From everything you've learned, which takeaway will stick with you?

"ACTION PLAN" ACTIVITY

Let's briefly work through the three steps of your action plan so you have concrete things to focus on as you apply the temperaments framework to your everyday life.

▶ Turn to the **Strength Training Tips** (pages 111–113) and choose two ways you'll work to stay in your strengths.

> **I will stay in my strengths by...**
>
> 1. _____ .
>
> 2. _____ .

▶ Turn to the **Scripture verses** (pages 115–117) and choose one verse that speaks to a weakness you'd like to work on. Copy it here.

> _____
>
> _____

▶ On the first line below, write the name of someone you'd like to build up with your words. Then turn to the **Build-Up Guide** (pages 119–123) for their temperament and choose one way you'll try to help with your words.

> **I'd like to build up** _____ ,
>
> **whose temperament is** _____ .
>
> **I'll do that by** _____ .

STRENGTH TRAINING TIPS

God wired you with the specific strengths of your temperament for a reason. He has perfectly equipped you for the purpose he's set for your life. Staying in your strengths unleashes the best, most authentic version of you. It's only from this place of health and strength that you're able to consistently speak helpful, life-giving words to others.

Use these tips to amplify the strengths you're naturally wired with.

SANGUINE STRENGTH TRAINING

Practice
▶ Pausing and filtering your thoughts before blurting them out
▶ Matching the volume and atmosphere in the room
▶ Remembering your obligations and establishing organizational systems
▶ Staying on track when telling a story
▶ Being on time and realistically assessing how long it will take to get there
▶ Waiting for the other person to finish talking and then asking them another question (instead of assuming control of the conversation again)
▶ Thinking before volunteering or committing to something (even if it sounds fun)
▶ Finishing what you start
▶ Telling only the truth and limiting your exaggerations
▶ Showing curiosity and interest in everyone (like trying to remember others' names)
▶ "Adulting"—being responsible for completing even the boring obligations like bills and errands
▶ Empathizing with others' emotions without trying to cheer them up or laughing them off

PHLEGMATIC STRENGTH TRAINING

Practice
▶ Regularly doing something—a class, hobby, or new skill—that interests you
▶ Advocating for yourself rather than letting resentment build
▶ Jumping into the conversation and sharing your ideas and opinions (even before you're asked)
▶ Matching the emotions and/or energy of others
▶ Trusting in your abilities and remembering the times you've succeeded in the past
▶ Responding enthusiastically
▶ Volunteering to be the leader, captain, or point person
▶ Committing to deadlines and meeting them
▶ Expressing your preferences when you're offered choices
▶ Explaining that you need time to think, rather than leaving others confused by your silence
▶ Sticking around until conflicts are fully resolved
▶ Vocalizing your admiration and/or appreciation of others (bonus if you do this directly to them)

CHOLERIC STRENGTH TRAINING

Practice
▶ Putting others first and verbalizing your appreciation for them
▶ Greeting others with a sincere smile and giving them your full attention
▶ Waiting until you're asked before sharing your opinions
▶ Listening all the way to the end—trying to understand, not just formulating your response
▶ Making requests instead of issuing demands; saying please
▶ Pausing for a deep breath when you feel yourself getting angry and/or loud
▶ Connecting with people, not just completing projects
▶ Moderating your tone and volume
▶ Owning your mistakes and apologizing out loud
▶ Praying for others instead of trying to fix them or giving them unsolicited advice
▶ Lightening up, cutting loose, stepping away from work and tasks, actually taking a vacation
▶ Giving others complete ownership over the method and time frame of completing tasks

MELANCHOLIC STRENGTH TRAINING

Practice
▶ Smiling more, lightening up, responding optimistically
▶ Being grateful and counting your blessings
▶ Reflecting back what others say to you to confirm that you heard correctly and completely
▶ Turning in/moving on from projects when they are good enough instead of trying to make them perfect
▶ Coming up with a Plan B when you start feeling anxious or overwhelmed
▶ Accepting invitations, joining in, volunteering
▶ Captivating your thoughts and memorizing helpful scriptural truths
▶ Responding with trust rather than suspicion (especially when there's a gap between what you expect and what you experience)
▶ Speaking up to share what's on your mind instead of withdrawing and isolating
▶ Being flexible, particularly about changes to your plans and/or schedule
▶ Sharing your creative talents and graciously accepting compliments
▶ Forgiving others and releasing grudges

SCRIPTURE VERSES
FOR YOUR TEMPERAMENT

Your temperament is neither a weapon nor an excuse. The temperament God wired you with contains weaknesses, but every conversation is an opportunity to overcome them. When your innate needs are unfilled, you can choose to fill them from your strengths rather than hurtfully resorting to manipulation.

Use these verses to stay focused on healthy ways you can grow.

SANGUINE VERSES

Encouraging Verses
Are not five sparrows sold for two pennies? Yet not one of them is forgotten by God. Indeed, the very hairs of your head are all numbered. Don't be afraid; you are worth more than many sparrows. (Luke 12:6–7)
Am I now trying to win the approval of human beings, or of God? Or am I trying to please people? If I were still trying to please people, I would not be a servant of Christ. (Galatians 1:10)
He chose us in him before the creation of the world to be holy and blameless in his sight. (Ephesians 1:4)
But you, Lord, are a compassionate and gracious God... abounding in love and faithfulness. (Psalm 86:15)
Cautionary Verses
The wisdom of the prudent is to give thought to their ways, but the folly of fools is deception. (Proverbs 14:8)
To answer before listening—that is folly and shame. (Proverbs 18:13)
A gossip betrays a confidence, but a trustworthy person keeps a secret. (Proverbs 11:13)

PHLEGMATIC VERSES

Encouraging Verses
Come to me, all you who are weary and burdened, and I will give you rest. (Matthew 11:28)
Make it your ambition to lead a quiet life: You should mind your own business and work with your hands... so that your daily life may win the respect of outsiders. (1 Thessalonians 4:11-12)
But the Lord said to Samuel, "Do not consider his appearance or his height...The Lord does not look at the things people look at. People look at the outward appearance, but the Lord looks at the heart." (I Samuel 16:7)
Blessed are the peacemakers, for they will be called children of God. (Matthew 5:9)
Cautionary Verses
Lazy hands make for poverty, but diligent hands bring wealth. (Proverbs 10:4)
Make every effort to keep the unity of the Spirit through the bond of peace. (Ephesians 4:3)
A sluggard's appetite is never filled, but the desires of the diligent are fully satisfied. (Proverbs 13:4)

CHOLERIC VERSES

Encouraging Verses

Commit to the Lord whatever you do, and he will establish your plans. (Proverbs 16:3)

Those who know your name trust in you, for you, Lord, have never forsaken those who seek you. (Psalm 9:10)

Whatever you do, work at it with all your heart, as working for the Lord... since you know that you will receive an inheritance from the Lord as a reward. (Colossians 3:23-24)

For you, [God], created my inmost being; you knit me together in my mother's womb. I praise you because I am fearfully and wonderfully made; your works are wonderful, I know that full well. (Psalm 139:13-14)

Cautionary Verses

Be completely humble and gentle; be patient, bearing with one another in love. (Ephesians 4:2)

When pride comes, then comes disgrace, but with humility comes wisdom. (Proverbs 11:2)

Those who trust in themselves are fools, but those who walk in wisdom are kept safe. (Proverbs 28:26)

MELANCHOLIC VERSES

Encouraging Verses

[God] gives strength to the weary and increases the power of the weak. (Isaiah 40:29)

But the Lord is faithful, and he will strengthen you and protect you from the evil one. (2 Thessalonians 3:3)

Therefore do not worry about tomorrow, for tomorrow will worry about itself. Each day has enough trouble of its own. (Matthew 6:34)

The Lord is my shepherd... He makes me lie down in green pastures, he leads me beside quiet waters, he refreshes my soul. (Psalm 23:1-3)

Cautionary Verses

Whoever listens to me will live in safety and be at ease, without fear of harm. (Proverbs 1:33)

May the God of hope fill you with all joy and peace as you trust in him, so that you may overflow with hope by the power of the Holy Spirit. (Romans 15:13)

Do not be anxious about anything, but in every situation, by prayer and petition, with thanksgiving, present your requests to God. And the peace of God, which transcends all understanding, will guard your hearts and your minds in Christ Jesus. (Philippians 4:6–7)

BUILD-UP GUIDE

The most significant impact of the temperaments framework is how it can improve your relationships. Knowing someone else's temperament is like having a cheat sheet! You know the four things they are wired to need, so you can choose your words accordingly. As the apostle Paul reminds us in Ephesians 4:29, speaking these helpful, life-giving words to others—speaking "according to their needs"—is always a win-win. It "benefits all."

Use these actions and words to build up others according to their temperaments' innate needs, and be alert for ways you may inadvertantly push them into their weaknesses.

SANGUINE BUILD-UP GUIDE

Build them up by...

▶ Listening to their stories.

▶ Making eye contact when they're talking.

▶ Being positive/matching their enthusiasm: *"It sounds like your day was awesome!"*

▶ Promoting their creativity: *"What should we do next? You pick."*

▶ Laughing with them.

▶ Showing interest in their friends: *"What's new with _____? I remember you telling me..."*

▶ Approving of them: *"You're so good at..."*

▶ Taking them seriously when needed: *"I can tell that upset you. You have every right to feel down."*

Caution! You may tear them down by...

▶ Being too serious: *"I just want to get this over with"* or *"Everything is ruined now."*

▶ Demanding perfection: *"Go back over this one more time."*

▶ Shaming them: *"Shhhh! You're being too loud"* or *"Stop. You're embarrassing me."*

▶ Consuming all their free time: *"This weekend we need to..."*

▶ Not listening or giving them your full attention.

▶ Not respecting their need for friends: *"Again? You're always going out with them!"*

▶ Requiring them to always be "on": *"What's wrong with you? Why are you so serious? Cheer up."*

CHOLERIC BUILD-UP GUIDE

Build them up by...

▶ Giving them something to be in control of: *"Will you be in charge of _____?"*

▶ Recognizing their work: *"That must have taken you hours! Thank you so much!"*

▶ Encouraging their intellect: *"You're great at solving this kind of problem. What do you think?"*

▶ Having their back: *"I know you have a good reason for..."*

▶ Letting them decide: *"Where should we eat? You pick."*

▶ Keeping communication short and to the point: *"Here's what you asked for."*

▶ Promoting their leadership: *"Why don't you lead out on this?"*

▶ Speaking logically and realistically: *"If..., then..."*

Caution! You may tear them down by...

▶ Making decisions for them: *"Here, this one's yours"* or *"Today we're going to..."*

▶ Not doing what you say you will do: *"Sorry, I didn't get around to it."*

▶ Embarrassing them in front of others (like with an overly emotional or unprofessional story).

▶ Arguing with or lecturing them: *"What makes you think you can...?"*

▶ Not asking for or respecting their opinions.

▶ Overlooking their work/assuming they'll do it: *"Why isn't the laundry done yet? You always do it."*

▶ Not verbalizing your appreciation for them/their strengths.

PHLEGMATIC BUILD-UP GUIDE

Build them up by...

▶ Letting them do one task at a time: *"If you could just do _____, that would be great."*

▶ Being kind in your criticism: *"Can I reflect something back to you?"*

▶ Asking their thoughts, opinions, and feelings: *"What sounds good to you?"*

▶ Showing curiosity about their interests: *"Tell me more about that. You're so good at it."*

▶ Encouraging their involvement: *"We'd love to have you join us!"*

▶ Listening completely, without interrupting.

▶ Giving them time to process: *"Think about it. We can talk more later."*

▶ Handling conflict calmly and quietly: *"Is now an okay time to talk?"*

Caution! You may tear them down by...

▶ Expecting things done in your time frame, not theirs: *"I thought you'd have this done by now!"*

▶ Pushing their involvement or interaction with others: *"You're going. I already signed you up."*

▶ Not listening when they speak up.

▶ Mistaking their quiet for apathy: *"Well, clearly this isn't important to you."*

▶ Speaking down to them: *"Do I have to do everything around here?"*

▶ Stressing them with expectations and orders: *"This has to be done now; we can't keep wasting time."*

▶ Not verbalizing their value—assuming they know how you feel about them, so you don't have to say it out loud.

MELANCHOLIC BUILD-UP GUIDE

Build them up by...

▶ Noticing when they need support: *"You must be slammed. How can I help?"*

▶ Keeping their secrets.

▶ Encouraging their creativity: *"I love seeing your artwork/hearing you sing/watching you play."*

▶ Being sensitive to their emotions: *"I can totally see why that made you sad."*

▶ Helping them feel safe: *"You can tell me anything. I'm always here for you."*

▶ Helping them formulate a Plan B: *"Okay, if that happens, what could you do instead?"*

▶ Making eye contact when they're talking.

▶ Believing in them: *"You've got this!"*

Caution! You may tear them down by...

▶ Dismissing their emotions: *"Lighten up, it wasn't that bad"* or *"Are you still not over that?"*

▶ Not giving them enough/all the details: *"Just ask around and see what you can come up with."*

▶ Infringing on their space and silence.

▶ Joining their complaining and judging: *"Ugh, that's the worst, isn't it? I hate it when..."*

▶ Changing the schedule—especially without notice: *"I told them we could meet for dinner."*

▶ Making them feel guilty or wrong: *"You never want to come with us."*

▶ Interrupting them.

Do not let any
unwholesome talk
come out of your
mouths, but only what
is helpful for building
others up according to
their needs, that it may

BENEFIT
THOSE WHO
LISTEN.

Ephesians 4:29

CLOSING WORDS

You probably engage in dozens of conversations daily, from logistical interactions like getting your kids out the door in the morning to emotional matters like being a sounding board for a friend. What you've learned over the last six sessions can dramatically influence every single one of those interactions.

You now *know better,* which gives you the opportunity to *do better.*

This is just the beginning of what I hope becomes a lifelong journey for you. It may be overwhelming or awkward at first. Translating the words that come naturally to you into the words that someone else is craving can be a little challenging. You won't always get it right. (I've spent almost three decades immersed in this material and I still stumble!) But your practice will pay off. In time, temperaments will go from something you do to someone you become.

God wired you perfectly. He wired *all of us* perfectly. I encourage you to use your words to reflect that beautiful truth to one another in every conversation you have.

Thank you for joining me. I'm honored to have started you on your journey.

Kathleen Edelman